Part-02

Bread Machine Cookbook

Learn How to Bake Delicious and Healthy Machine Recipes for Beginners. Start Baking Your Own Gluten-Free Bread and Enjoy Your Homemade Loaves, Buns, Pizza & Dough.

NYDIA WISE

Table of content

Part 6: One Push to Perfect Bread Machine

Today we are going to learn about one post perfect bread machine. In this lesson, we are going to learn some recipe item and some bread item. I hope all things were looking good because we are describing it about so, first of all, we are making almost 7th chapter in this lesson. Search on sorry please read all seven chapters correctly, and you would see some Bate recipe which is very important for this book. So why we are waiting for let's start from the first chapter.

Chapter I: Everyday Bread:

Today is our first chapter name being everyday bread. In this lesson, we are learning how much and how many more significant we can make every day and which is very useful for every people who are already making those kinds of bread every day. Because we are people, we need to eat breakfast or something for eating. So, there are all kinds of recipe that we are mentioned in this book lesson by lesson. I hope after reading this paragraph for reading this article, you also can understand which bread is preferred for you, and which not so you can realize your recipe correctly. So, let's start it.

Soft White Bread:

Now let's learn about soft bread recipes so that we can make it for our in-home by bread-making machine.

To make this simple recipe, first, add the yeast.

Dilute a little sugar in warm water, and sprinkle with the active dry yeast all over the face.

The water should be warm but not hot. Consider the temperature at which you can bathe a baby- it is a little warmer than the temperature. If the water is too hot, it can kill the yeast; then your bread will not rise.

After about 5 minutes, the yeast will have melted, and the mixture will look like foam. This shows how your yeast is working on time.

Add about 2 cups of flour, and butter.

When everything is set, mix another 1/4 to 1/4 cup of flour, and salt. You should first see the dough forming on the ball, then move from the sides of the bowl neatly.

Serve in another 1/2 cup of flour, kneading until the bread feels smooth and stretchy. It provided an excellent long bend (about 10 minutes) to improve the texture of the bread.

Now place the pan in a bowl with a small non-stick spray, and toss the dough again. Cover it with plastic and let it rise in a warm place until it is twice as big. This will usually take anywhere from 30 to 45 minutes.

When the dough has risen, knead it and knead it a few times, forming a loaf of bread.

Place the uncooked dough in a loaf pan and cover with a non-stick coating paper.

This will require another 30 to 45 minutes to get up a second time, then go into the oven until golden brown and puffy.

And here it is with your recipes for white bread. I hope with this step you can make it your own.

Mediterranean Bread:

Now let's learn about Mediterranean Bread recipes so that we can make it for our in-home by bread-making machine.

Time: 3hrs 15mins

APPLICATION: 5

UNITS: US

Ingredient:

- 1 1/2 PROVINCIAL TABLET
- 5/8 cup water
- 1/4 cup devours feta cheese
- 1 7/8 clove garlic, ground
- 7/8 teaspoon of salt
- 5/8 teaspoon honey
- 5/8 tablespoon virgin olive oil
- 2 1-16 cups flour flour
- 1/3 cup chopped kalamata olive
- 1 1/4 teaspoon dried oregano
- 1/2 teaspoon of yeast or 1/2 teaspoon yeast that rises quickly

POINTS

Measure the ingredients in the baking pan in the order recommended by the manufacturer.

Place the pan in the oven chamber.

Select Basic Cycle; press to start.

When the baking cycle is over, quickly remove the bread from the pan and place it on a rack.

Allow cooling to room temperature before cutting.

FOOD INFORMATION

Service Size: 1 (102) g

Services per Recipe: 8

AMT. PERFORMANCE ----------------- % OF TOTAL DAILY

Calories: 237.4

Calories from Fat 40 g---------------- 17%

Total fat 4.5 g ----------------- 6%

saturated fat 1.4 g---------------- 6%

Cholesterol 5.6 mg---------------- 1%

Sodium 497.3 mg -----------------20%

Total Carbohydrate 42.4 g -----------------14%

Dietary Fiber 1.9 g ----------------7%

Sugar 2.6 g ----------------10%

Protein 6.5 g ----------------12%

Light Rye bread:

Now let's learn about Light Rye bread recipes so that we can make it for our in-home by bread-making machine.

INGREDIENTS

- 1 cup of water
- 1 1/2 teaspoon salt
- Two tablespoons sugar
- One tablespoon butter or vegetable oil
- Two teaspoons caraway seeds
- 2 cups bread flour
- 1 cup rye flour
- 1 1/2 teaspoon yeast for yeast

POINTS

Place all the ingredients in a loaf pan.

Choose a loaf of basic bread, 1.5-pound bread in the size of the bread and between the colour of the crust. Press Start. When done, remove the bread from the baker and carefully remove the mixing lump from the bottom of the loaf.

Allow cooling for 10 minutes before cutting with a bread knife.

Serve: 12

Whole Wheat Bread:

Now let's learn about Whole Wheat Bread recipes so that we can make it for our in-home by bread-making machine.

Ingredients

- 1 1/4 cups lukewarm water
- Two tablespoons olive oil or vegetable oil
- 1/4 cup honey or maple syrup
- 3 1/2 cups King Arthur White Whole Wheat Flour, Premium Whole Wheat Flour, or Organic Whole Wheat Flour
- 1/4 cup sunflower, sesame or flax seeds, or a mixture, voluntarily
- One tablespoon of wheat gluten, optional; high rise
- 1 1/2 teaspoon salt
- 1 1/2 teaspoons instant yeast

Instructions

1. Bread machine instructions:
2. To make bread in a loaf of bread: Put all the ingredients in a loaf pan in the order in the list. The basic white bread plan (or whole wheat bread, if your machine has a full-grain area), then press start.
3. Remove the bread from the machine when you are done. It's either taking it out of the pan and into the rack to cool it; or remove it from the pan, put it back on the machine (on top of the structure holding the pan), break the lid open for about 1 ", and let it cool directly on the floor cooler. This helps prevent the crust from wrinkles as the bread cools.

Handmaking:

1. Combine all ingredients in a large bowl, or a stand mixer.
2. Knead the dough until smooth and lightly browned, about 8 to 10 minutes.
3. Place the dough in a greased container, cover, and allow to rise to double in volume, approximately 1 to 1/2 hours.
4. Gently roll out the dough and shape it to fit an 8 1/2 "x 4 1/2" loaf pan. Let it rise, cover, and double, about 1 to 1 1/2 hours.
5. Bake the bread in a preheated oven at 375 ° F for 35 minutes, or until a digital thermometer is placed in the centre of the oven at 190 ° F.
6. Remove the bread from the oven, remove from the pan, and relaxed in a storage area.

Egg Bread:

Now let's learn about Egg Bread recipes so that we can make it for our in-home by bread-making machine.

Eggs bring a lot to this or any bread recipe.

First of all, eggs bring color, nutrition and added flavor to any bread recipe.

Eggs also contain lecithin. That's the oil that makes the ingredients blend better and gives the bread a delicious crumb.

Whole eggs are watery. So, if you are trying to add eggs to the recipe, make sure you prepare the liquid in the recipe to compensate.

Ingredients

- 1/3 cup water
- 3/4 cup milk
- Two eggs - beaten
- 4 cups bread flour
- Two tablespoons olive oil
- Three tablespoons sugar
- 1 teaspoon salt
- 1 1/4 teaspoons dry yeast active

Instructions

Follow the instructions that come with your bread machine as to what ingredients you should put in the bread machine first. With my machine, I inject the liquid first.

Use the basic bread setting, and I chose the "medium" for the crust preparation.

Look at the dough after five or ten minutes of mixing. Just pop on top of the bread machine and see how the dough works. It should be a smooth, round ball.

The 2-lb bread:

Now let's learn about the 2-lb Bread recipes so that we can make it for our in-home by bread-making machine.

Time: 3hrs 10mins

APPLICATION: 12

UNITS: US

INGREDIENTS

- 1 1/2 cups of water
- 2 tablespoons canola oil
- 1 3/4 teaspoons of salt
- 4 cups bread flour
- 2 tablespoons sugar
- 2 1/4 teaspoons dry yeast active

POINTS

1. Measure and place the liquid ingredients in a baking pan.
2. Measure and grease in a baking pan.
3. Measure and add the dry ingredients (without yeast) to the baking pan.
4. Sprinkle the yeast over the flour.

5. Add a baking pan to the bakers and close the lid.
6. Select "Basic" settings.
7. Select the "Light" color setting.
8. Press to start.
9. Remove the baking pan after about 55 minutes of baking time.
10. Gently stir the bread from the baking pan into the cooling area.
11. If necessary, remove the bread crumbs. Be careful; it's hot!
12. Set the bread straight, cover with a towel and simmer for 20 minutes.

Your recipes are done.

Chapter II: Healthy Bread

We already finished chapter one we are beginning to chapter 2. in this chapter, we all learn about the healthy bread. have some question do you know what is healthy bread. If you think this is, then you are perfect because a healthy bread is that bread which has a loss of nutrition. And before this chapter we also already learn about the nutrition bread and how can we increase nutrition so in this chapter we all are going to show some nutritious Bread recipe, which is very important and it is very heavy for healthy. Let's begin and learn some more recipe about the bread machine.

Making Lower Carb Bread:

Now let's learn about Making Lower Carb Bread recipes so that we can make it for our in-home by bread-making machine.

This delicious and fragrant recipe for Low Carbohydrate Bread Machine Bread will surely delight people who enjoy their bread.

Preparation time 10 minutes

Course: Advertisement, side

Cuisine: American

Search Results: bread, low carb

Services: 12

Resources: Bread Machine

Ingredient:

- 1 cup Water Heating Water Heater
- 1 ½ tbsp Sugar
- 1 ½ tsp Bread Machine Bread
- 3 cups Cabrioles
- 3 tsp Vital Wheat Gluten
- ¼ cup of vegetable oil

Instructions

1. Lightly spray your pan to prevent sticking. Start by making yeast by placing warm tap water, sugar and yeast in a pan and allowing it to evaporate. It should take eight to ten minutes before it starts buzzing.
2. Add the remaining ingredients and set the baking machine to bake in primary mode if you don't have a low carb mode.
3. Enjoy your bread!

Cooking Notes

As mentioned, you will need the yeast of the bread machine. This is a different type of yeast than the yeast you are currently using. You will also need Vital Wheat Gluten (this is not a gluten-free recipe). Lastly, you will need low carb flour. I know there are many options out there, including the gluten-free type. I'm very confident in something like Carbalose flour.

Gluten-Free Bread

Now let's learn about Making Lower Carb Bread recipes so that we can make it for our in-home by bread-making machine.

An easy way to make a delicious gluten-free bread ... on the bread machine!

Dry Ingredients

- 3 cups of gluten-free nutritional flour (I use Orgran product or Mixed Flour Free DIY Gluten)
- 2 tablespoons sugar
- 1 teaspoon of xanthan gum
- 1 teaspoon salt
- One sack (7 grams) of dried yeast

Wet Ingredients

- 1 ½ cups of almond milk (or preferred milk)
- ¼ a cup of olive oil
- 3 eggs - medium
- 1 teaspoon white vinegar

Methods:

1. Mix all the dry ingredients in a bowl.
2. In another bowl, combine all the wet ingredients until combined.
3. Put the wet ingredients in the breadcrumbs pan.
4. Spoon the dry ingredients over the water.
5. Mix the dry and wet in a bread pan.
6. Turn on the bread machine and bake in the primary setting. (My machine takes 3 hours and 5 minutes.)
7. When the bread is done, leave the bread in a loaf pan for 15 minutes and then go to cool.

Vegan Bread:

Now let's learn about Vegan Bread recipes so that we can make it for our in-home by bread-making machine.

Definition

A perfect egg-free, gluten-free, dairy-free and allergen-friendly recipe that will do the prepping and baking of your next fermented bread!

Keep in mind that every loaf of bread is different, so you may need to play around with your settings. Of all the methods I've tested, I use only the set placement in the mine to create the best bread!

You will not need a bread mixer for this recipe. Use only the bread machine for baking your bread.

Ingredients

- 1 cup buckwheat flour
- 1/2 cup white rice flour
- 1/2 cup brown rice flour
- 1/2 cup tapioca flour *
- 1/2 cup potato starch
- 1/2 cup seed or nut flour **
- 1/2 teaspoon acceptable sea salt
- 1 teaspoon palm coconut sugar (or maple syrup)

- Two tablespoons husky psyllium
- 2 teaspoons active yeast
- One cup of warm water ***
- 11/ 4 cup homemade hemp milk ****

Instructions

Step 1

Before you start, be sure to weigh and filter all the dry ingredients. This step is essential to avoid small lumps of starch or flour in your bread.

Step 2

Mix warm water, yeast and psyllium husk in a large bowl and mix gently. You can wait 5 minutes or continue adding to all remaining dry ingredients. Also, to ensure that all your ingredients are correctly sorted, you can place the filter on top of your mixing bowl and, at the same time, add the dry ingredients. Remove the sieve and gently mix the ingredients. Add the hemp milk and continue mixing until all the dry and wet ingredients are well incorporated; we do not want to leave any dry pieces of flour.

Step 3

You can let the dough rise directly into the mixing bowl or transfer the mixture to a bread machine pan. Cover and rise in a warm place for 2-5 hours or until the dough has grown to more than an inch in height or doubled in size.

Step 4

When ready to bake, gently roll out the dough in a bread pan, if not, and bake for at least an hour and 10 minutes. You will only use the baking setting on your bread machine.

Step 5

Your machine should ring when the bread is finished baking. When the bread is ready, you will need to remove it from the pan and allow it to cool completely for a few hours in a cool place. Cut and enjoy!

Last Tip

Once down, the bread will finally be neatly wrapped in a clean tea towel for one day. You can cut and store the leftovers in the fridge for up to five days or freeze the pieces to keep them longer.

Resources: Bread machine.

Notes

* Arrowroot starch flour is an excellent substitute for tapioca flour.

** I have tried green sunflower, pumpkin, and Baru seed flour and I have also tried almond flour for food. Use almond flour only if you are not infected.

*** For the best bread, please use chlorine-free water. Filtered and spring water works very well.

**** You can try other types of plant-based milk. I often use hemp milk as it is allergen-friendly and is a delicious ingredient in 2-ingredient milk made at home. To make your hemp milk, mix 1/3 cup of organic hemp seeds with 1-1 / 4 cups of water and mix it with a blender that blends well until white and hard. Pour the hemp milk into a mesh bag or a good vegetable filter to remove large unwanted pieces.

Important:

Make sure the ingredients you buy are prepared in an area free of the high allergens you are avoiding. Gluten-free products should be certified and clearly labelled. Contact your doctor about your diet.

Low-Fat Bread:

Now let's learn about Vegetarian Bread recipes so that we can make it for our in-home by bread-making machine.

This recipe should work in machines that will make two kilograms of bread. For best results, add ingredients in the recommended sequence to your machine manual.

Ingredients

- 1 7/8 cups water or chickpea broth (aquafaba)
- 4 2/3 cups whole wheat white flour
- Four tablespoons essential wheat gluten
- 2 tablespoons sugar
- 1 1/2 teaspoon salt (1 tsp. When salted aquafaba is used)
- 2 1/2 tablespoon high-speed yeast (2 tsp. Dry yeast that works if fast rotation is not used)

Instructions

Place the water or chickpea broth in a bread pan. Add the remaining ingredients to the order listed (or as recommended by the manufacturer of your bakery.) Please make sure the yeast does not mix with the liquid by placing it in an external source on top of the ingredients.

Choose either a fast-baked wheat cycle (use 2 1/2 tsp. High-speed yeast) or a regular wheat cycle (use 2 tsp. Active dry yeast). Press to start. Remove the bread when the baking is done. The bread will be well separated if allowed to cool first.

Notes

Make sure all ingredients are in room temperature.

Add the flour before mixing. Use nesting cups and spoon flour into cups up to the top—level by sweeping up with a knife.

The bread will be cut better when it cools down.

The difference

To make straightforward bread, you can replace whole wheat flour with whole wheat flour. Use these measurements:

1 2/3 cups water or aquafaba dry yeast active if you use a regular cycle)

Preparation time: 10 minutes | Cooking time: 2 hours (s) 25 minutes (s) Number of resources (yield): 12

Nutrition (per activity): 134 calories, six calories in fat, <1g total fat, 0mg cholesterol, 221.5mg sodium, 154.6mg potassium, 27.6g carbohydrate, 4.4g fibre, 1.7g sugar, 6.5g protein

Chapter III: Specialty Bread

We all already Finnish learning from Lesson 2. now we are starting to learn from lesson 3. and you can tell chapter 3 also. So in this chapter, we are going to learn specialty bread. I hope we also understand to see the title because it's all about the specialty. There are so many kinds of recipe that we are going to mention in this lesson. I hope by regarding this you can learn more knowledge about Lesson 3. this is one kind of learning experience, so let's know the weekend to start.

Danish Dough:

This simple Danish recipe is a great way to start with the oily dough. This, in particular, requires only a few days to complete. The most important thing to remember is that a cake can smell scary. Bc sure! You are the boss! Now, own the dough.

Make enough dough for 24 small Danish

Ingredients

- 1 cup whole warm milk (105 ° F to 110 ° F)
- 2 tablespoons and 2 teaspoons (24 grams) active dry yeast
- 4 cups (563 grams) flour for all purposes
- ⅓ A cup (67 grams) of powdered sugar
- ¼ cup (57 grams) butter-free butter, soft
- 1 tablespoon orange zest
- 1 teaspoon (9 grams) kosher salt
- 3 large eggs

Instructions

In a small bowl, place the warm milk; sprinkle yeast on top. Let stand until the mixture has bubbled, 7 to 10 minutes.

In a bowl of stand mixer mixed with the dough, beat the flour, sugar, butter, zest, and salt on low heat until combined, 2 to 3 minutes. Add the mixture of yeast and eggs, beat until combined.

Roll out the dough in a cool place, then knead 2 to 3 times until a smooth ball form. Firmly wrap the plastic wrap, and refrigerate for at least two hours or overnight.

Frosted Cinnamon Bread

Ingredients

- 1 cup warm milk (70 ° to 80 °)
- 1/4 cup water (70 ° to 80 °)
- 1/4 cup butter, soft
- 1 large egg
- 1 teaspoon salt
- 4 cups bread flour
- 1/4 cup vanilla pudding quick mix
- 1 teaspoon sugar
- 1 tablespoon active dry yeast
- 1/4 cup butter, soft
- 1 cup full of brown sugar
- 2 teaspoons ground cinnamon

BEATING

Nine ounces of cream, soft

- 1/4 cup butter, soft
- 1.1/ 2 cups confectioners sugar
- 1.1/ 2 teaspoons milk
- 1/2 teaspoon extracted vanilla

Directions

1. In a breadcrumbs pan, place the first nine ingredients to lift through the elements. Select dough setting (check the dough after 5 minutes of mixing; add 1-2 tablespoons of water or flour if needed).
2. When the cycle is complete, roll out the dough into a flour-free place. Roll into 17x10-in. Rectangle. Spread with butter; sprinkle brown sugar and cinnamon. Roll up, jelly-roll style, starting on the long side; press the seam to mark. Cut into 21 pieces.
3. Place 12 slices, cut sideways, in a 13x9-in fitted baking pan and nine rolls in 9-in. square baking pan. Cover; let rise in a warm place until doubled, about 45 minutes.
4. Bake at 350 ° for 20-25 minutes or until golden brown. Cool on rack racks for ten minutes.
5. In a large saucepan, whisk the ingredients until smooth. Warm rolls of snow. Store in the refrigerator.

Pumpkin Bread

This delicious pumpkin bread made from a bread machine makes another delicious and colorful daily white bread. It can make a great match with a warm bowl of celery or baked beans for a special treat.

In this recipe, you can use your mashed pumpkin or canned pumpkin puree. This can be a fair use of your jack-o-lantern if you are willing to apply elbow grease for cooking and baking. See the recipe for crockpot pumpkin puree if you want to go the route to start with the whole pumpkin.

One cup of pumpkin, as included in this bread, contains 171 per cent of the daily amount of vitamin A, as well as vitamin C. You will be adding nutritious food to your bread. No spices are included in this recipe, so it is not bread with pumpkin spices. If you want to add something, that's your choice.

You can enjoy your spiced pumpkin bread with butter or margarine or plain. In addition to enjoying chilli, soup, or stew, try frying it for breakfast. It should be delicious with apple butter and other spiced spices. It does not have its spices, so it will depend on what is best.

Ingredients

- 1/2 cup and 2 tablespoons milk (5 ounces)
- 1 cup grated pumpkin (or canned pumpkin puree
- 4 cups bread flour
- 2 tablespoons vegetable oil
- 2 tablespoons sugar
- 1 1/4 teaspoon salt
- 2 1/4 teaspoons dry yeast active

Steps to Take

1. Add all the ingredients according to your suggested bread maker order, by default be the order listed in the list of ingredients above.
2. Use white bread suspension, light crust.
3. Alternatively, if you want to use a faster cycle on your bread machine, use 3 teaspoons of faster / more rapid yeast and choose a medium crust.
4. Let your machine do its thing and enjoy the bread when it is ready.

Babka Bread:

ender and fluffy, and full of cinnamon flavour! Our Bread Machine Cinnamon Babka recipe makes this delicious, twisted bread very easy to assemble.

Production: 1 (9x5 bread)

Preparation time: three hours

Cooking Time: 45 minutes

Total time: 3 hrs. 45 minutes

Course: Bread Food: Middle East

Services: 8 people

Ingredients

For Dough

- ¾ c milk, heated to 80-90F
- 2 ¼ tsp (one packet) active dry yeast
- 4 Tbsp salted butter
- 3 Tbsp sugar
- 2 egg yolks (keep whites, separately, see below)
- 1 tsp pure vanilla
- 2 eggs (complete)
- 3 ½ - 4 c whole-grain flour
- 1 tsp salt

Filling

- 1 c brown sugar
- 1 Tbsp cinnamon
- Salt tsp salt
- 2 Tbsp melted butter melts and cools
- 1 egg white (see above)

Egg bath

- 1 egg white (see above), beaten lightly

Instructions

Dough (Type of Bread Machine)

1. In a small saucepan, combine warm milk and yeast. Put this mixture aside for 5-10 minutes, until the yeast starts to explode.
2. While the yeast starts, cream the butter and sugar and the electric hand mixer in a medium bowl. Add the egg yolks, one at a time, beating between each egg. Add the vanilla and all the eggs, one at a time, whisking each in half. Set this mixture aside.
3. Serve the yeast mixture, and place it in a loaf of bread (lined with dough). Pour the egg and butter mixture over the milk.
4. Add 3 cups of flour and salt.
5. Start your bread machine in its Dough Cycle. Watch your dough as it begins to stir. When it looks like the ingredients are thoroughly mixed, add more flour, ¼ cup (or less) at a time, allowing the machine to mix between each insert, until the dough is combined and then from the sides of the bowl.
6. When the dough comes off the sides of the bowl, please turn off your bread machine and let the machine run into its Dough Cycle. When the cycle is complete, you want the bread to be about twice as large.

For the Dough (Stand Mixer Version)

1. In a small saucepan, combine warm milk and yeast. Put this mixture aside for 5-10 minutes, until the yeast starts to explode.
2. While the yeast starts, whip the butter and sugar together in a bowl of your stand mixture, topped with pads, at medium speed. Add the egg yolks, one

at a time, beating between each egg. Add the vanilla and whole eggs, one at a time, beating in the middle of each filling.

3. Serve the yeast mixture, then place in a bowl with your butter and egg mixture. Combine integration.
4. Add 3 cups of flour and salt. Stir in the pad attachment, until the ingredients are combined, then switch to your dough hook.
5. Mix the dough at medium speed with the dough hook. Add the flour, ¼ Noma cup (or less) at a time, until the dough comes together and starts from the sides of the bowl. Continue to bake for 5-8 minutes, until the dough is very smooth.
6. Transfer the dough to a clean, greased container and cover the bowl loosely with plastic wrap. Set the dough in a warm, unfinished place to rise until it doubles, 1 - 2 hours.

Filling

As the dough thickens, make the filling by beating all the filling ingredients together in a medium bowl, until smooth. Set aside.

All Inclusion

1. Grease a 9x5 loaf pan and load it with greased parchment paper.
2. Roll the dough from its growing container to a fine flour.
3. Throw the dough on the floor and roll it into a rectangle about 18x15 inches.
4. Spread the filling evenly over the dough, leaving a 1-inch border on the long sides.
5. Roll out the dough, starting at one of the long sides.
6. Cut the roll in half, length, and turn it into two strands.
7. Cut the two strands together, trying to keep the cut (filling shown) side at the top, as far as possible.
8. Finally, roll out your twisted dough into 8 pieces, and keep the cut sides as high as possible. Place this twisted figure 8 in a greased and line-filled loaf pan.
9. Cover the dough in a pan loosely with plastic wrap and rise for 30 minutes.
10. After 30 minutes, preheat your oven to 350F.
11. When the dough has risen slightly and looks puffy, remove the plastic wrap and brush the top of the dough with a white egg yolk.
12. Bake the bread at 350F for 45-55 minutes, until the top layer is deep golden and the bread feels empty when you tap. (The internal temperature of the bread should be read about 180F when the bread is made). (It would be

helpful to place a piece of aluminum foil or aluminum sheet made with a baking tray on the rack under the bread to hold any filling out of my box.)

13. Once the bread is done, cool the bread in the pan for 10 minutes, before gently removing the bread from the pan to continue to cool for 10-20 minutes before cutting.

14. The babka will remain freshly placed in a waterproof container at room temperature for 3 days, then transfer the bread to the refrigerator.

Challah:

Ingredients

- ¾ cup milk
- 2 eggs
- 3 tablespoons margarine
- 3 cups flour flour
- ¼ A cup of white sugar
- 1 ½ teaspoon of salt
- 1 ½ active teaspoons dry yeast

Directions Checklist

Step 1

Put the ingredients in a pan in the bread machine in the order suggested by the manufacturer.

Step 2

Select basic bread settings and Light Crust. Get started.

Honey Hawaii Bread:

Ingredients

- Juice pineapple juice for a cup
- 1 egg
- 2 tablespoons olive oil
- 2 Spoon milk
- 2, teaspoons of sugar
- Salt a teaspoon of salt
- 3 cups flour flour
- 1 ½ active teaspoons dry yeast

Instructions

1. This makes two kilograms of bread. Follow the instructions that come with your bread machine as to what ingredients you should put in the bread machine first. (My bakery recommends adding drinks first.) Use a primary setting.
2. I make my own with a loaf of bread placed in the centre. It turned out a little darker than I would have liked. Next time I will use the bright light setting.
3. Look at the dough after five or ten minutes of mixing. It should be a smooth, round ball. When very dry, add a teaspoon of liquid at a time until it looks just right. If it seems too wet, add a tablespoon of flour at a time until it looks just right. Most of the time, however, the above values should be correct.

After long research, we already understand about the bread-making process, and we also know so many recipes, so in this lesson, we all are learning some easiest and fast recipe so that we can make some recipe very quickly and very fast. We are trying or ways to give some recipes among them. So please don't waste it time left it to start it.

Banana Bread:

Using a bread machine makes baking banana easier than before. The bread processor helps to make the banana bread soft, delicious and allows it to remain utterly wet throughout the process. It's a great way to use ripe bananas without opening the oven, so your kitchen stays cool.

Bananas bread is a quick bread recipe, which means you don't add yeast. Instead, baking powder and baking soda are yeast-based additives that are used to rise faster than required for yeast bread. Using a bread machine, you make a process that is almost completely removed with a tiny device: almost everything mixes directly in the baking pan.

Every loaf of bread is different, so it is essential to follow the instructions of the model manufacturer who owns it to ensure success. Also, make sure that the bread machine is ready to operate before you start mixing. Once the wet and dry ingredients are incorporated into the pan, they need to be mixed and baked immediately. Many have a quick bread setting, or some people use their instant system or manual settings. At the end of the cycle, you can always use a toothpick to check your bread supply and bake it for a while if it is not cooked correctly.

Ingredients

- 2 large eggs (room temperature)
- 1/3 cup butter (room temperature)
- 1/8 cup milk (room temperature)
- 2 medium bananas
- 1 1/3 cups bread flour
- 2/3 cup sugar
- 1 1/4 teaspoons of baking powder
- 1/2 teaspoon baking soda
- 1/2 teaspoon of salt
- 1/2 cup carved (lightly smeared)

Steps to Take

1. Combine ingredients.
2. Put the eggs, butter, milk and bananas in a bread pan and set aside.
3. In a medium mix, combine the remaining dry ingredients.
4. Mix well and place in a bread pan.
5. Use a quick (or equivalent) bread setting for your machine. When you are done baking, remove the pan from the device. Let the bread sit for about 10 minutes, then remove it from the pan and set the bread on the rack to cool. Enjoy!

Soda Bread:

Raisins and caraway seeds may sound like a weird blend, but the effect is perfect on this updated bakery version of the classic recipe.

Ingredients:

- 2-1 / 2 teaspoons dry yeast
- 3 tablespoons milk butter
- 3 cups white bread flour
- 1/2 teaspoon baking soda
- 1 teaspoon salt
- 2 tablespoons sugar
- 1 teaspoon caraway seeds
- 1/2 cup dried
- 2 tablespoons melted butter
- 1 cup of warm water

Preparation:

1. Set your bread machine with white bread, if applicable.
2. Put all the ingredients except the dried grapes in your bakery container in the prescribed order. Dried should be added after the first mixing.
3. Follow the manufacturer's instructions.

Cornbread:

Cornbread is one of the oldest bread recipes, and this version is an old-fashioned combination. You can finish it in the bread machine or pour it into a baking dish or cake pan to make each serving.

This is an old blend of pepper, soup, stew and fried foods from chicken to fish. Good and alone with a soft touch of butter.

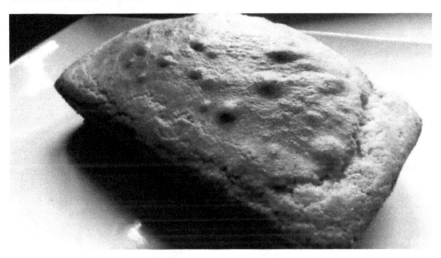

Ingredients:

- 1 cup of flour
- 1.25 cups flour
- 4 tsp baking powder
- 0.25 cup sugar
- 1 tsp salt
- 1 tsp vanilla
- 2 eggs - lightly beaten
- 1 cup of milk
- 0.25 cups melted butter or oil

References:

1. Put the ingredients in the order shown and select the cake setting. If your machine does not have a cake setting, you can always choose the oven option shown above.
2. When the cornbread is done, let rest for 10 minutes and cut and serve.

Toasted Coconut Bread:

Ingredients

- 1¼ cup (about the ounces) of sugar-free coconut
- 1 1/8 half and a half cups (regular or non-fat)
- 2 large eggs
- ¼ canola oil
- Two teaspoons extracted coconut
- 1 teaspoon vanilla extract
- ¾ cup of sugar
- 2 cups not added flour for all purposes
- 1 tablespoon baking powder
- Salt a teaspoon of salt
- 1½- or 2-pound loaf machines

Instructions

1. Preheat the oven to 350 ° F.

2. Sprinkle the coconut on a non-stick baking sheet and toast in the oven until lightly browned, about three minutes. Transfer quickly to a small bowl and allow to cool to room temperature.

3. Place the ingredients in a pan according to the manufacturer's instructions, add the coconut with the dry ingredients. Set the crust to black, if your machine provides crust control for this setting, as well as the Quick Bread / Cake cycle; press Start. The batter will be thick and smooth. When the machine rings at the end of the process, check the bread to see if it has delivered. The bread is made when it is slightly reduced from the sides of the pan, the sides are dark brown, and the top is firm with gentle pressure when touched with your finger. The toothpaste or metal will come out clean when placed in the middle of the bread.

4. Once the bread is done, quickly remove the pan from the machine. Let the bread stand in the pan for 10 minutes before turning it off, on the top right side, so that it is completely relaxed in the oven before cutting. Fold tightly wrapped in plastic wrap and store at room temperature.

Oatmeal Walnut Bread

This classic oatmeal bread recipe is perfect for a good lunch Ishi sandwich... and oatmeal bread adds healthy oatmeal to your family's diet. Because this recipe does not contain powerful spices, this old oatmeal bread can be used for a wide variety of lunch sandwiches like ham & cheese sandwiches, chicken sandwiches, beef sandwiches, etc. Please visit Bread Bread (BreadDad.com) for great bread recipes.

Ingredients - Recipe Machine Oatmeal Bread Recipe - 1.5 lb Bread Bread

- 1 Cup - Milk (lukewarm)
- 3 teaspoons - unsalted butter (cut)
- 2 1/4 Cups - Flour Bread
- 3/4 cup - Old Fashioned Oatmeal (not fast oatmeal)
- 1/4 cup - Brown (whole) sugar - If you choose non-sugar oatmeal loaves, you should use only 1 teaspoon of brown sugar.
- 1 1/2 teaspoon - Salt
- 1 1/2 teaspoons - bread machine yeast

Services - About 12 pieces

- Materials needed for this recipe - Measuring cup and spoons, flexible spatula, oven meter, rack rack ... and of course, a bread machine!

Instructions - Recipe Machine Oatmeal Bread Recipe

1. For 2 lb. bread, please use a 2 lb. ingredient list and set the bread machine settings to 2 pounds of bread, light color and "basic" bread options. For 1.5 lb. bread, please use the 1.5 lb. ingredient list and set the bread machine settings to 1.5 pounds of bread, light color and "basic" bread options. FYI - Make sure you do not mix the 1.5 lb. & 2 lb. ingredient with the machine settings!
2. Put all the ingredients that start with milk in a "bucket" (bread pan). Make sure the yeast retains and does not touch the milk or salt. Some people like to make a small "divot" on top of the flour to hold the yeast in one place before the machine starts.
3. Connect the bread machine. Enter the appropriate settings (either 1.5 lb or 2 lb version) and press the "start" button.
4. Options - After the breadcrumbs have finished baking and before the start of the baking cycle, sprinkle the old oatmeal flakes over the bread dough.
5. When the loaf is finished baking, remove the loaf. Remove the bread and place in a cool place. Use the mitts of the oven when removing the bread from the oven (bread pan) because it will be too hot!
6. At our Sunbeam Bread Machine, baking takes about three hours for two kilograms of bread (and 2:53 hours for 1.5 lb. bread) in a light color and basic bread settings. However, some appliances may be different, and you do not want to be away from home when the alarm machine "stops" off! Your bakery should show you the length of baking time after setting the settings in the device. This will allow you to know when to be in the kitchen to remove the bread.
7. Before using your bread machine, you should read the manufacturer's instructions on how to use the bread machine effectively and safely.

In this chapter, we are learning about some sweet bread recipes with ingredient and instruction. I hope we also can learn something about it.
Let's start learning.

Chocolate Bread:

Ingredients

- 1 packet of yeast bread
- 3 cups flour
- 2 tablespoons brown sugar
- 2 tablespoons granulated sugar
- 1 teaspoon salt
- 1 teaspoon cinnamon ground
- Four tablespoons softened butter
- 1 egg, beaten lightly
- 1 cup warm milk
- 1/4 cup water
- 1 cup of chocolates

References

1. Combine all ingredients except the chocolate chip in the bread machine as directed by the machine maker. Choose white bread, light crust.
2. If the machine has the notice to add nuts or other add-ins, add chocolate chips immediately. Otherwise, add them before the final round of mixing.
3. Once the bread is baked, remove the pan from the machine and allow the pan to cool on a wire rack for 5 minutes. Remove the bread from the pan and allow the bread to cool completely on a wire rack.
4. Store bread in a waterproof container for 3-4 days at room temperature, or let it stand for two months.

Sweet Rolls bread:

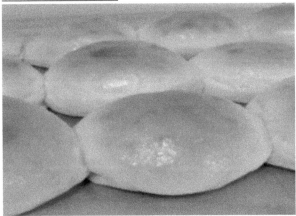

Ingredients

- 1 1/3 c milk (1 c. And two t. Milk)
- 4 Tbsp sweet butter
- 1 large egg, beaten lightly
- 1/3 c sugar
- 1 tsp salt
- 4 c all-purpose white flour, filtered
- 2 tsp dry active yeast
- Egg washing
- 1 egg
- 2 Tbsp milk

Disclaimer:

- Place the dough ingredients in the machine in sequence, cover the liquid ingredients with flour and add the last yeast. When you have finished the dough cycle, roll out the dough, dividing it into 12-18 equal pieces (depending on how much you want your rolls to roll) for the best way to build your volumes, watch the video.
- Place on a lightly greased baking sheet, cover and fold in until doubled. I baked this in two different types of baking pans: 8-inch perimeter and 9x13 sheet. The 8 inch round makes them more than a "Pull A Part roll", and you have to bake for a while. The 9x13 bakes them everywhere and comes out very nice. I prefer 9 x 13.

Cheesy Bread:

INGREDIENTS

- 3/4 cup water, room temperature
- 1 large egg
- 1 tsp salt
- 3 cups flour flour
- 1 cup shredded sharp cheddar cheese
- 2 tbsp dry milk
- 2 tbsp sugar
- 1 tsp yeast for yeast

PREPARATION

STEP 1

Put the ingredients in a bread pan in the order recommended by the manufacturer, add the cheese and flour.

Recommended cycle: Basic / white bread cycle; medium / normal color setting. Do not use a delayed baking feature.

To fix the consistency of the dough: After mixing for a few minutes, the ingredients should turn into a smooth ball around the kneading blade. If the dough seems too thick or too soft, add more liquid or flour to 1 teaspoon increments, until the right consistency is reached. Do not add more than 3 to 4 teaspoons juice or flour. The machine cannot afford a wide variety and may not be able to bake a large dough properly.

Garlic Bread

Ingredients

- 1 cup water (70 ° to 80 °)
- 2 tablespoons and 1-1 / 2 tablespoons butter, softened
- 1 teaspoon honey
- 2/3 cup grated Parmesan cheese
- 1.1/ 2 teaspoons of garlic powder
- 3/4 teaspoon of salt
- cups flour
- 1.1/ 4 active teaspoons dry yeast

Directions

1 In a loaf pan, place all the ingredients in the order suggested by the manufacturer. Choose essential bread preparation. Choose crust colour and bread size if available. Bake according to the instructions of the bread machine (check the dough after 5 minutes of mixing; add 1 to 2 tablespoons of water or flour if necessary).

2 Freeze option: Wrap securely and freeze the cooled bread in foil and place in a commercially available plastic refrigerator bag. To use, melt at room temperature.

Chapter VII: Traditional Bread

In this chapter, we all are learning about some traditional Bread. In there we added some conventional recipes so that you can also make it in your home to read it. Let's know and enjoy.

Country Bread:

This simple recipe for white bread crumbs makes for a soft loaf of bread with a delicious, chewing texture. It's a delightful breakfast drink or used to make sandwiches, from an old turkey club to a final cheesecake cheese. This white bread does not have many air holes or blisters, and the taste and texture are amazing

You can make this bread in a quick or quick cycle, but it can also be made in a regular round with a little yeast (about two teaspoons).

Ingredients

- 1/2 cups water (lukewarm)
- 1/2 cups flour made for the whole purpose
- 1 cup bread flour
- 1/4 teaspoon baking soda
- 2 1/2 teaspoon yeast for yeast
- 1 teaspoon and 1 teaspoon olive oil
- 1 1/2 teaspoons sugar
- 1 teaspoon salt

Steps to Take

- Combine ingredients.
- Put all the ingredients in your bread pan in the order recommended by the manufacturer of your bakery. Set in the quick or quick setting with the central crust. Push the start.
- When ready, turn the bread in a row to cool.
- Cut and enjoy.

Sour Dough

INGREDIENTS

- 1 cup to start the sourdough dough
- 1 ½ cups of warm water
- 1 ½ teaspoon of salt
- ½ A cup of white sugar
- ½ corn cup oil
- 6 cups flour flour

Directions

1 Mix sugar, corn oil, salt, water, and one cup to start the sourdough dough together in a large bowl. Whisk in the flour and add to the mixture. Grease or oil the dough. Place the dough in a greased container, cover, and rise overnight.

2   The next day, knead the dough for 10 minutes. Divide in half, then place 4 x 8-inch bread pans. Allow the dough to double in size.
3   Bake at 350 degrees F (175 degrees C) for 40 to 45 minutes, or until the bread is golden brown and then tap a little. Turn cool on wire racks.

Appendix 1:

Sizing Your Bread:

So, we all understand how to use a bread machine and how to make bread on it. And also understand so many recipes in this eBook. Now it's time to learn sizing your bread. It's one of the processes in bread. You make bread in the machine now you need to cut to for eat. So you have to remember the need to size it with a sharp knife and make then slide by slide so that it looks good when you want to make some decoration on it.

Being Waste-Aware:

We make bread and also size it with a sharp knife, but you have to be aware when you want to eat it, don't waste any bread. Because it's eating instrument, so you have to be very knowledgeable whey you want to eat it.

How to Use Old Bread

There have so many ways to use old bread. You can also make recipes with it, and even if you want, then you can make it a toast with bread toaster. So please don't waste any bread, use every single part of it. I hope it's essential to use your old bread correctly.

Appendix 2:

How to Enjoy Your Bread

In appendix II, I am going to teach you how to enjoy your bread. First of all, I want to tell you enjoyment is all about depends on itself. Because if you're going to make a bread that you can use it, and we were telling you all the source that we have. and make sure easiest recipe and most popular recipe nutrition for the recipe and the most valuable recipe we all are mature in this book. So, this is the time to enjoy your bread. Before enjoying it, we also tell you how to cut it and how to slice it. But one thing here to realize if you want to eat something for your food family like a party dinner then you can use with bread also cheese Mozzarella and food that well with bread. We also can use a food flavor that is very important because we all are one to eat extracurricular activities with the great, so before this great, you can give some jelly. And you can also use some sauce that you make it in your home; you can buy from the store. But all about you can mix it to eat your bread.

Remember eating purpose is always was peoples to you because this is great and you know how it was and white for definitely for eating so you can use your flavour, and on I tend to eat it as your satisfaction.

I hope this book is delightful for you and you also enjoy every writing from here and also learn so many things because from top to bottom we all talk about for various thing, first of all, we talk about the machine how it works and how to do it works. Then we talk about the ingredient, and we also tell you how the element is most important and if you want to be a master class in a breath then what you want to do have to most professional with scale. We also tell you how you have to be your best friend with a plate and why it is essential. Then we show you some bread items and how a machine works and where the music is happening in lost something we offer you in this book. And in the next steps, we are sharing some recipe with their ingredient and the process to make it. There are almost many many recipe hair that we are mentioning in this so I hope that you can use it and you can try it in your home, enjoy your bread.

This is your life because you all know how a bit machine works and how to make any kinds of the recipe using this machine without a long time. I hope this book helps you so much to increase your knowledge and increase your it and saving time. This is all about for today. Thank you very much for reading this book. Good job and let's enjoy life.

Thank you

CPSIA information can be obtained
at www.ICGtesting.com
Printed in the USA
BVHW091505150221
600148BV00002B/55

9 781801 548205